>YOU+DO-THE-MATHS

Use your maths skills to catch the criminal.

POLICE LINE DO NOT CROSS

SOLVE A CRIME

HILARY KOLL AND STEVE MILLS

ILLUSTRATED BY VLADIMIR ALEKSIC

QED

Created for QED Publishing, Inc. by Tall Tree Ltd
Editor: Jon Richards
Designers: Ed Simkins and Jonathan Vipond
Illustrator: Vladimir Aleksic

QED Editorial Director: Victoria Garrard
QED Art Director: Laura Roberts-Jensen
QED Editor: Tasha Percy
QED Designer: Krina Patel

First published in the UK in 2014 by
QED Publishing
A Quarto Group company
The Old Brewery
6 Blundell Street
London, N7 9BH

www.qed-publishing.co.uk

A catalogue record for this book
is available from the British Library.

ISBN 978 1 78171 695 3

CONTENTS

Hi, my name is Alex and I'm a plain-clothes police detective. I'm here to show you how maths can help you solve a crime.

Words in **bold** are explained in the glossary on page 32.

TYPES OF CRIME

You have been chosen to lead a team of detectives who are investigating a burglary at a block of flats.

Crimes are known as criminal offences and there are many different kinds. Two main types are 'offences against people' and 'offences against property'.

Offences against people include assault and robbery. Offences against property include crimes such as arson and burglary.

You are studying a newspaper article showing crime figures from the past 30 years.

Monday 4th May 2015

Falling crime!

It is estimated that there were eight million incidents of crime in the 12 months to the end of September, with violent offences dropping by 13 per cent and overall household crime, including burglary, falling by one tenth. Crimes against people were down nine per cent. Vehicle theft was down by a quarter. Murders and killings have almost halved in the last decade.

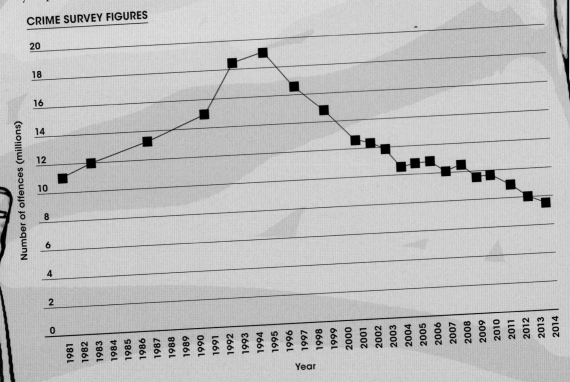

CRIME SURVEY FIGURES

Number of offences (millions) vs Year

1 a) The crime report says that there were eight million incidents of crime. Write eight million in figures.

b) Murders and killings have almost halved. Write one half as a **fraction**, as a **decimal** and as a **percentage**.

CRIME FALL	FRACTION	DECIMAL	PERCENTAGES
Violent offences	¹³/₁₀₀	0.13	13%
Murders and killings	¹/₂		
Household crime	¹/₁₀		
Vehicle theft	¹/₄		
Crimes against people			9%

2 Copy this table and add in the missing fractions, decimals and percentages.

3 If there were 96,000 vehicle thefts last year and this has gone down by one quarter, how many were there this year?

4 If there were 5,400,000 household crimes last year and this has gone down by 10 per cent, how many were there this year?

WHAT ABOUT THIS?
If 20 per cent of the eight million incidents were offences against people, and 80 per cent of the eight million incidents were offences against property, how many of each type were there?

POLICE DETECTIVES

Your first role is to pick your team of investigators – they'll need to do a number of different jobs from senior officers to regular policemen and women, as well as specialist roles, such as forensic experts.

Those applying to join your team must be in good health and be physically fit.

They should also have a Body Mass Index (BMI) between 18 and 30.

This table shows five people who would like to join your team.

NAME	M/F	WEIGHT	HEIGHT
Dan Archer	Male	80 kg	2 m
Iain Jones	Male	140 kg	2 m
Alice Raven	Female	45 kg	1.5 m
David Singh	Male	90 kg	2 m
Paula Lee	Female	64 kg	1.6 m

1 Of the group of five, who is:

a) the shortest?
b) the lightest?
c) the heaviest?

2 How many centimetres taller is:

a) Dan than Paula?
b) David than Alice?

David

Dan

Paula

Alice

Body Mass Index (BMI) is used to see if a person is overweight or not. It is calculated using this **formula** (weight in kilograms and height in metres):

BMI = (weight ÷ height) ÷ height

3 Use the formula to help you find the BMI (in kg/m²) of:

a) Dan b) Iain.

4 To find the BMI of the others, it can be easier to think of their heights as whole numbers and to multiply by 100.

a) Alice (45 ÷ 15) × 100 ÷ 15 = ?
b) David (90 ÷ 20) × 100 ÷ 20 = ?
c) Paula (64 ÷ 16) × 100 ÷ 16 = ?

WHAT ABOUT THIS?
Which of the five people have a BMI between 18 and 30?

SCENE OF THE CRIME

After arriving at the block of flats, your first job is to cordon off the area so that no one can disturb any evidence.

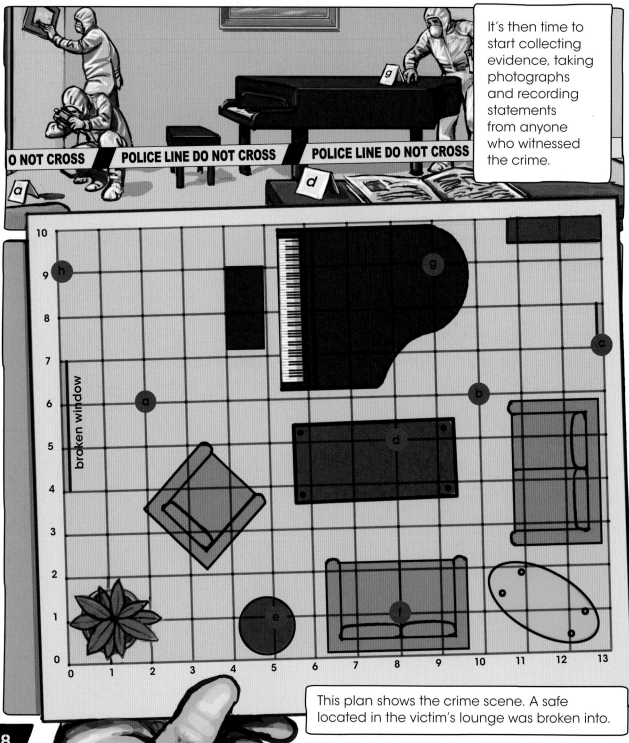

It's then time to start collecting evidence, taking photographs and recording statements from anyone who witnessed the crime.

This plan shows the crime scene. A safe located in the victim's lounge was broken into.

ITEMS FOUND	LABELLED
drop of blood	a
broken vase	b
safe door	c
newspaper	d
mobile phone	e
set of keys	f
glove	g
picture on wall	h

1 The places where pieces of evidence were found have been labelled on the plan. Give the **co-ordinates** of each item.

EVIDENCE EVIDENCE EVIDENCE EVIDENCE

2 Describe which items of furniture each of these things were found on or near:

a) a pen was found at (13, 5)
b) a mug was found at (12, 1)
c) an elastic band was found at (1, 1)
d) a knife was found at (4, 3).

50 cm
50 cm

3 Each square on the plan represents 50 cm in real life. What is the distance, in metres, between:

a) a and b? b) d and f?
c) g and h? d) e and f?

WHAT ABOUT THIS?
Items d, e and f are at the corners of a triangle. If the distance in real life between d and e is 2.5 m, what is the **perimeter** of the triangle in real life?

FORENSICS AND FINGERPRINTING

Your forensics team arrives at the crime scene to collect detailed evidence. Forensic experts check the scene of the crime to look for fingerprints and other tiny bits of evidence to help identify the criminal.

Fingerprints come in several different types, although no two people have exactly the same prints. Forensic experts brush a light powder over prints to make them visible.

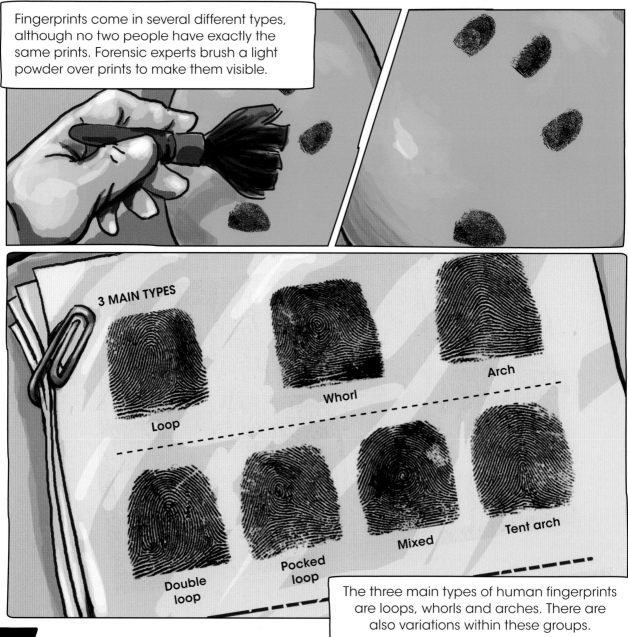

3 MAIN TYPES

Loop

Whorl

Arch

Double loop

Pocked loop

Mixed

Tent arch

The three main types of human fingerprints are loops, whorls and arches. There are also variations within these groups.

This **pie chart** shows the approximate proportions of each fingerprint type that would be expected in a group of people.

Arches
$^1/_{20}$

Whorls
$^3/_{10}$

Loops
$^2/_3$

1 There are 60 people in a room.

a) Find $^1/_{20}$ of 60 to find out how many people you would expect to have arches in that room.

b) Find $^3/_{10}$ of 60 to find out how many people you would expect to have whorls.

Whorls
$^3/_{10}$

Loops
$^2/_3$

2 There are 300 people in a concert hall. Using the fractions on the pie chart, how many of these people would you expect to have:

a) loops? b) whorls? c) arches?

3 Add your three answers together. What do you notice?

4 Find $^{13}/_{20}$ of 300 and compare it with $^2/_3$ of 300. What do you notice? Why is this?

WHAT ABOUT THIS?
Find out what type or types of fingerprints you and your friends or family have. Look on the internet for more information about identifying your type. What proportions of different fingerprint types do you all have?

DNA

Your forensic team collects DNA samples from the crime scene. DNA is a spiral-shaped chemical that is found in every cell of the body.

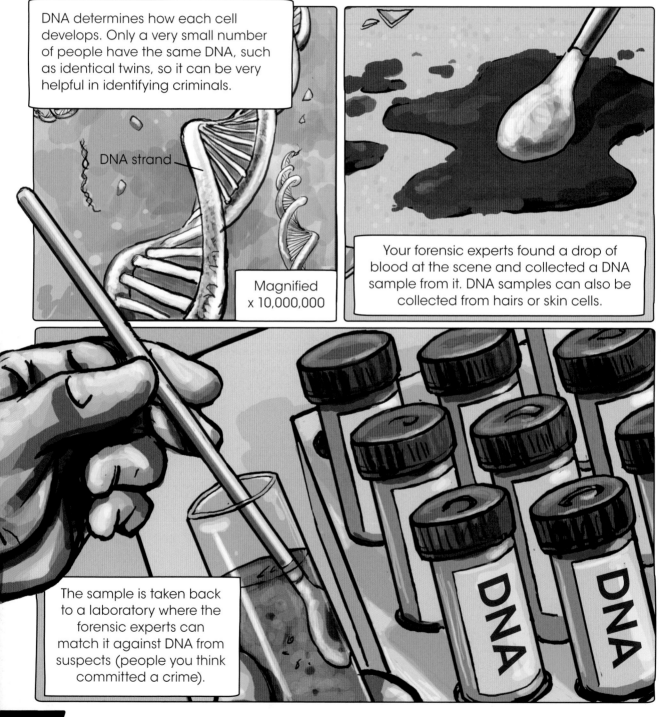

DNA determines how each cell develops. Only a very small number of people have the same DNA, such as identical twins, so it can be very helpful in identifying criminals.

DNA strand

Magnified x 10,000,000

Your forensic experts found a drop of blood at the scene and collected a DNA sample from it. DNA samples can also be collected from hairs or skin cells.

The sample is taken back to a laboratory where the forensic experts can match it against DNA from suspects (people you think committed a crime).

DNA

DNA

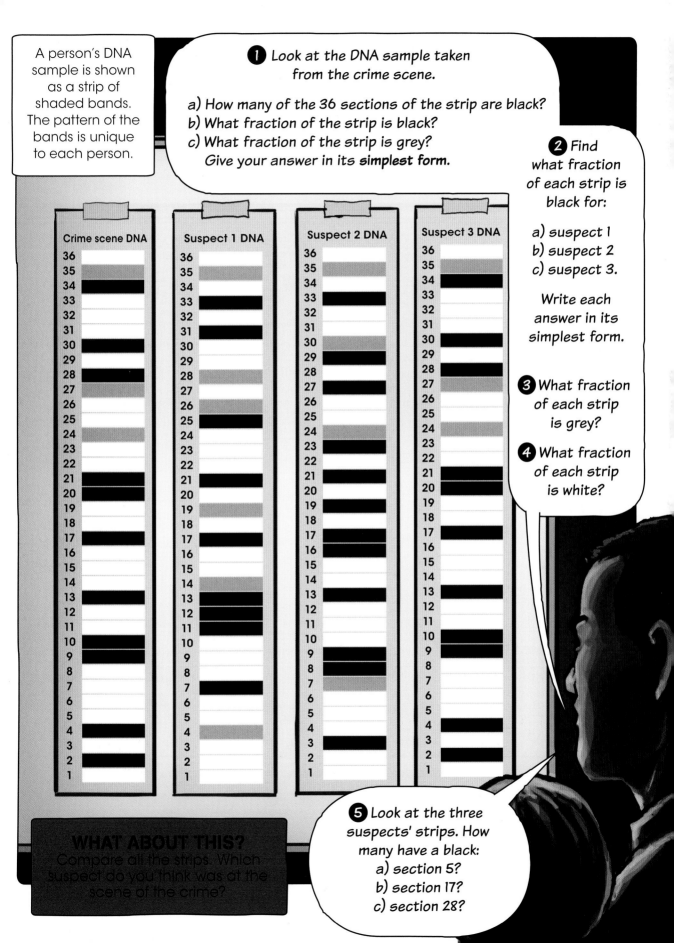

TIMELINES AND ALIBIS

Collecting evidence and taking statements from witnesses allows you to put together a **timeline** of events showing when things happened.

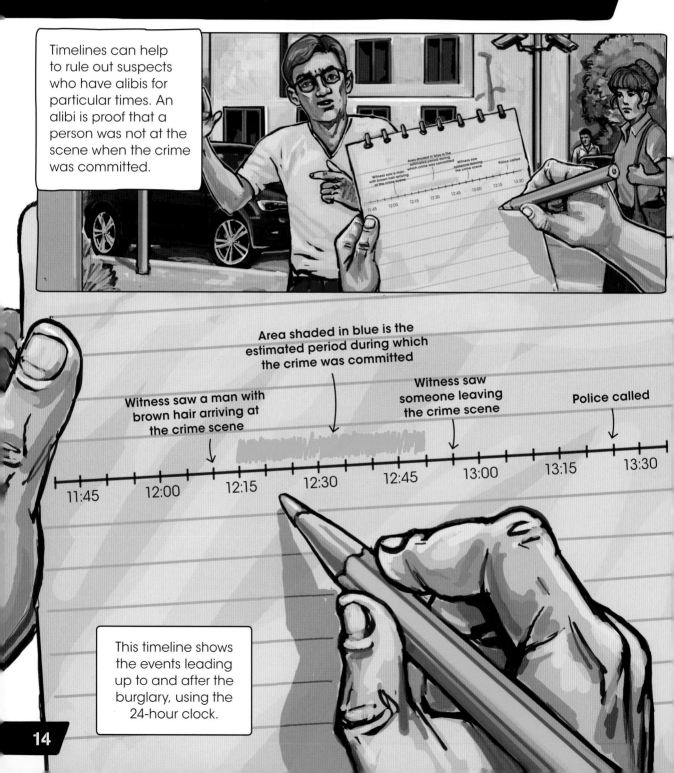

Timelines can help to rule out suspects who have alibis for particular times. An alibi is proof that a person was not at the scene when the crime was committed.

Area shaded in blue is the estimated period during which the crime was committed

Witness saw a man with brown hair arriving at the crime scene

Witness saw someone leaving the crime scene

Police called

11:45   12:00   12:15   12:30   12:45   13:00   13:15   13:30

This timeline shows the events leading up to and after the burglary, using the 24-hour clock.

1 Give your answers using the words 'past' or 'to'. At what time:

a) did the witness see a person arriving at the crime scene?
b) did the witness see a person leaving the crime scene?
c) were the police called?

3 How long:

a) is the estimated period?
b) was the person at the crime scene, according to the witnesses?
c) after the person was seen leaving were the police called?

Estimated period during which crime was committed

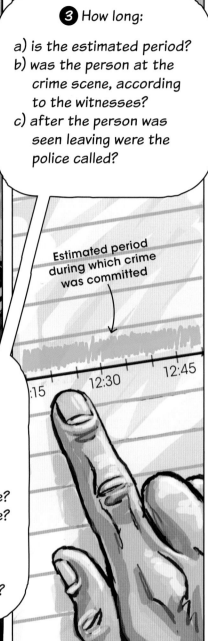

:15   12:30   12:45

2 Using the period shown on the timeline, could the crime have been committed at:

a) noon?
b) half past twelve?
c) five minutes past twelve?
d) ten minutes past twelve?
e) twenty minutes to one?
f) five to one?
g) one o'clock?
h) twenty-five past twelve?

WHAT ABOUT THIS?
Three suspects have alibis that confirm their whereabouts at the following times:

Suspect 1: from eleven-thirty until five to one.
Suspect 2: from midday until quarter past one.
Suspect 3: from one o'clock until half past two.

Write whether each suspect could have committed the crime based on their alibis.

CAMERA FOOTAGE

One other thing your team must check is the footage from security cameras near the crime scene.

Camera footage is often useful in providing evidence that a person was at or near a crime scene. Detectives will look at video footage from any cameras near the scene.

Crimes themselves are sometimes captured on camera and footage can be used in court as evidence.

This plan shows the car park outside the block of flats where the burglary took place. The blue shaded sections are the areas covered by the CCTV cameras at 1, 2, 3, 4 and 5.

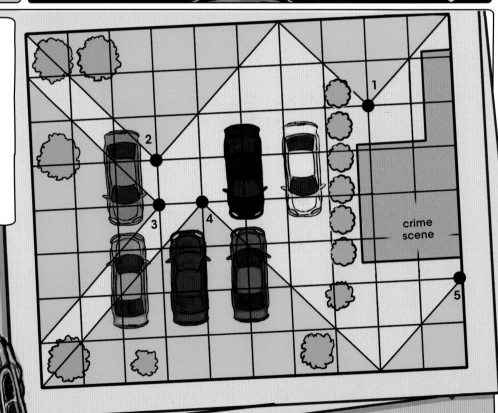

POLICE

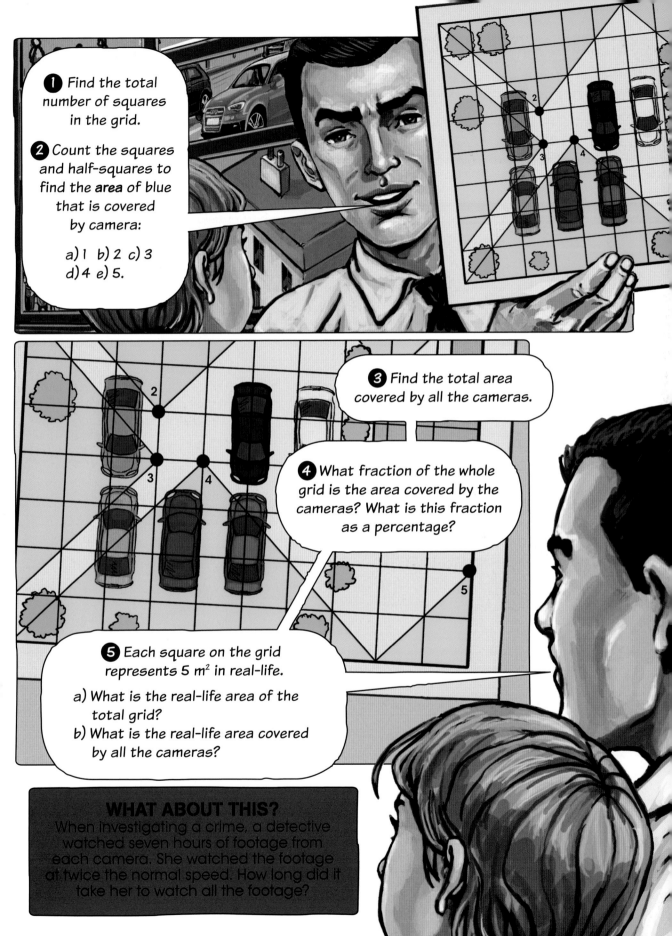

VITAL EVIDENCE

One of your detectives is keeping a record of what has happened and when during the investigation.

This record will help you to keep track of when and where any evidence is found and recorded.

2.00 pm

2.30 pm

4.45 pm

TIME	ACTIVITY
2:00 pm	Arrive at the scene of the burglary
2:15 pm	Secure the perimeter
2:30 pm	Talk to the victims
3:40 pm	Talk to witnesses
4:15 pm	Process scene, including videoing & photographing
4:45 pm	Collect evidence
6:00 pm	Transport evidence for analysis
6:35 pm	Return to police station

This table shows what the detective did during his initial investigation.

TIME	
2:00 pm	Arrive at the scene o...
2:15 pm	Secure the perimete...
2:30 pm	Talk to the victims
3:40 pm	Talk to witnesses
4:15 pm	Process scene, inc...
4:45 pm	Collect evidence
6:00 pm	Transport evidenc...
...m	Return to police...

2 Write how many minutes the detective spent from the start of each activity below, to the start of the next activity:

a) securing the perimeter
b) talking to the victims
c) talking to witnesses
d) collecting evidence.

1 Write in words the time (using the words 'o'clock', 'past' or 'to') that the detective:

a) arrived at the scene of the burglary
b) began to talk to witnesses
c) began to collect evidence
d) returned to the police station.

3 What was the detective doing at:

a)
b)
c) 16:05
d) 17:37

WHAT ABOUT THIS?
If the detective began work at 9:00 am and, on returning to the police station after being at the crime scene, he stayed another 25 minutes before finishing work, how many hours did he work in total?

SURVEILLANCE

Surveillance officers watch people or places to gather information to help solve crimes or to get enough evidence for a court case.

You have received a tip-off that the suspect is going to be in a café nearby.

You send an undercover surveillance officer to sit outside the café and record the number of people entering. She estimates the age of each person and makes a note of their hair colour.

This is her recording sheet.

GENDER	M	F	F	M	F	F	M	M	M	F	M	F	M	M
AGE	20s	50s	20s	30s	60s	70s	30s	30s	40s	40s	50s	20s	20s	40s
HAIR COLOUR	Bl	Br	Blo	Bl	Br	Br	Blo	Rd	Bl	Br	Bl	Bl	Bl	Rd
GENDER	M	M	F	F	F	F	M	M	M	M	F	F	M	F
AGE	80s	40s	60s	20s	50s	70s	30s	40s	50s	30s	40s	20s	30s	60s
HAIR COLOUR	Bl	Rd	Br	Rd	Blo	Br	Bl	Br	Br	Br	Bl	Blo	Rd	Br

Key for hair colour   Blo = Blonde   Bl = Black   Br = Brown   Rd = Red

MALES		
ESTIMATED AGE	TALLIES	FREQUENCY
20s		
30s		
40s		
50s		
60s		
70s		
80s		

1 The data is reorganized into two frequency tables (one for males and one for females). Copy the table then complete the tallies to find the frequencies.

2 How many males appeared to be:
a) in their 20s? b) in their 70s?
c) in their 50s? d) in their 30s?

FEMALES		
ESTIMATED AGE	TALLIES	FREQUENCY
20s		
30s		
40s		
50s		
60s		
70s		
80s		

3 How many females appeared to be:

a) in their 40s? b) in their 80s?
c) in their 60s? d) in their 20s?

4 How many more males were there than females in total?

WHAT ABOUT THIS?
The tip-off said the suspect was going to the café with a man in his 50s who has brown hair. Describe two possible suspects using the data from the recording sheets.

PROFILING

To help solve your investigation, you turn to the help of a criminal profiler. Trained in human behaviour, profilers analyze the evidence from the crime, and make predictions about the characteristics of the unknown criminal.

Profilers look for motives – reasons why someone might commit a crime.

A criminal profiler has said that the suspect is likely to be a man in his 30s, with no educational qualications, who probably has his own vehicle. You have put together this list of possible suspects.

NAME	SEX	AGE	LEVEL OF EDUCATION	OWNS OWN VEHICLE?
Simon Stone	M	37	None	Y
John Cox	M	34	GCSEs	N
Sam Evans	M	51	Degree	N
Urvi Chandi	M	42	None	Y
James Jones	M	36	None	Y
Mel Mason	M	47	A levels	Y
Chris Carter	M	37	None	Y
Joe West	M	44	GCSEs	N
Richard Reed	M	48	A levels	N
Tom Collins	M	39	Degree	Y
Toby Franks	M	50	Degree	N
Ed Lodge	M	42	None	Y
Arthur Holt	M	41	GCSEs	N
Hugh Na	M	63	Degree	Y
Richard Fox	M	53	GCSEs	Y
Paul Raven	M	42	None	N
Larry Jones	M	39	A levels	Y
Simon Dupa	M	49	GCSEs	Y

1 How many of the men in the list:

a) own their own vehicles?
b) are in their 40s?
c) are between 38 and 52 years old?
d) have a degree qualification?

2 Do any men in their 40s have a degree? What if you widened the age range to 38 to 52?

3 List the names of any men between 38 and 52 with a degree.

4 How many men in their 40s have qualifications listed as 'A levels'? How many of them have a vehicle?

NAME	SEX	AGE	LEVEL OF EDUCATION	VEH...
Simon Stone	M	37	None	Y
John Cox	M	34		N
Sam Evans	M			N
Urvi Chandi	M			
James Jones	M			
Mel Mason	M			
Chris Carter	M			
Joe West	M	48	Degree	
Richard Reed	M	39	Degree	Y
Tom Collins	M	50	None	N
Toby Franks	M	42	GCSEs	Y
Ed Lodge	M	41	Degree	Y
Arthur Holt	M	63	GCSEs	N
Hugh Na	M	53	None	Y
Richard Fox	M	42	A levels	Y
Paul Raven	M	39	GCSEs	
Larry Jones	M	49		
Simon Dupa	M			

WHAT ABOUT THIS?
Looking at the table, make a list of the suspects who are in their 30s, have no educational qualifications and own their own car.

E-FITS

With the help of witness statements, your next task is to put together an E-fit, or a picture of the suspect's face, based on the witnesses' recollections.

An E-fit is constructed using computer software to build up different parts of a person's face.

Two witnesses have given you slightly different descriptions of what the suspect may have looked like. You have put together these two E-fits using different eyes, noses and mouths.

Suspect A

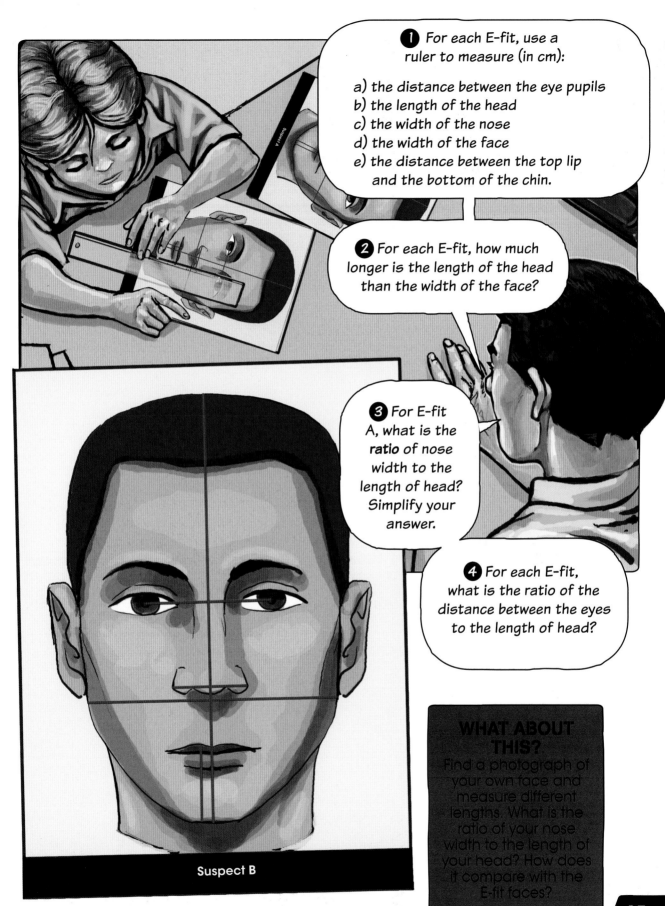

SOLVING THE CRIME

The victims of the burglary tell the detectives that
£1600 in cash was stolen from the safe.

The detectives decide to check the suspects' bank accounts to see if any large amounts of money have been paid in.

Sometimes, criminals pay in money in small amounts over several months to avoid suspicion.

1 How much would a suspect pay in altogether if he paid:

a) £300 per month for 3 months?
b) £900 per month for 7 months?
c) £110 per month for a year?
d) £70 per month for 11 months?
e) £80 per month for 18 months?
f) £70 per month for 2 years?

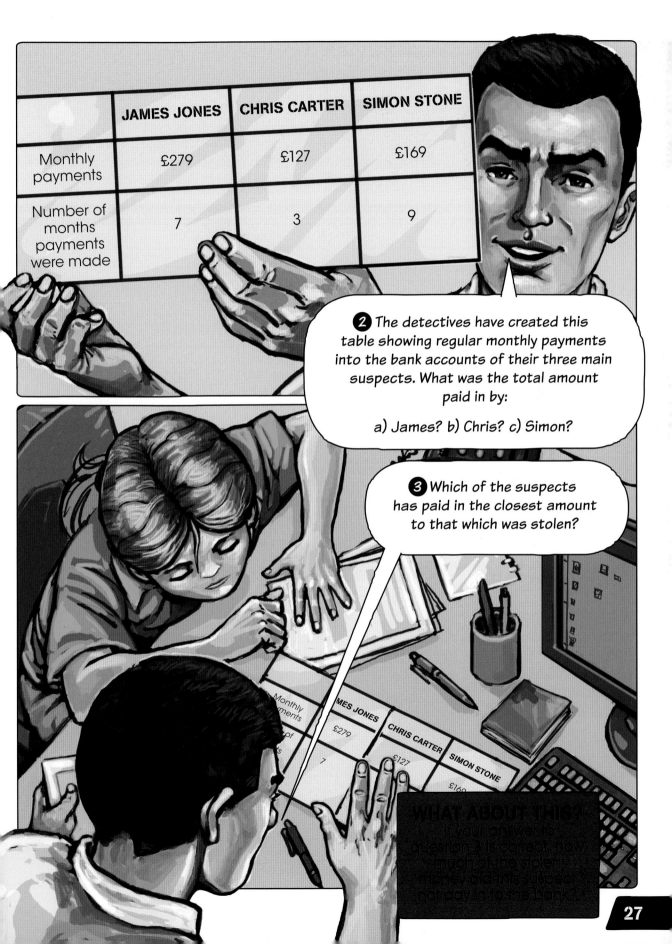

THE ARREST

Your investigation is reaching its climax! DNA tests from the crime scene and other evidence have confirmed the identity of the criminal.

Now that you've solved the crime, it's time to go and arrest him. He has been reported as being in a blue car travelling east along Green Lane (marked with a blue circle below).

The eastern end of Green Lane is closed due to roadworks so he's in a traffic jam.

① You leave the police station car park (marked with a P). Describe two different routes to reach the suspect's car (blue circle). Use compass directions in your descriptions.

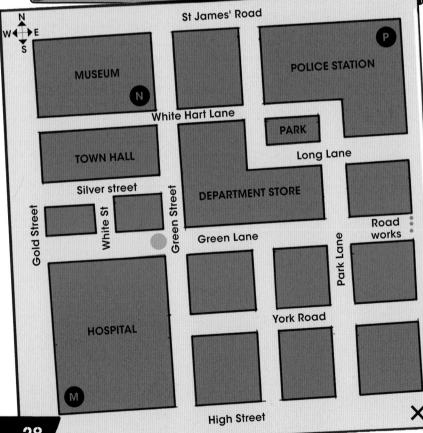

2 You reach the suspect's car, but it's parked and he's escaped on foot! You know that the suspect owns a storeroom (marked N) near the Museum. How many different routes are there to get from the blue circle to N using only streets with a colour in their name.

3 You receive a tip-off that the suspect ran north along Green Street and then east along White Hart Lane. Where could he be hiding?

You're still inspecting the car but you're told that the suspect's moved again and he's now running along the eastern end of High Street. You rush to make the arrest (at the black cross).

4 How many different routes are there from the blue circle to the black cross, avoiding the road-works?

Arriving at the end of High Street, you spot the criminal and make the arrest!

WHAT ABOUT THIS?
The suspect is first taken to the hospital for treatment to a cut and is then taken to the police station to be charged. Are there more or fewer than 20 possible routes from M to P on the map?

ANSWERS

Congratulations! Your team has solved the crime and caught the criminal! Check your answers here and see how well you did.

PAGES 4–5

1. a) 8,000,000 b) ½, 0.5, 50%

2. 0.5, 50; 0.1, 10%; 0.25, 25%; 9/100, 0.09

3. 72,000

4. 4,860,000

WHAT ABOUT THIS? There were 1.6 million crimes against people and 6.4 million against property.

PAGES 6–7

1. a) Alice b) Alice c) Iain

2. a) 40 cm b) 50 cm

3. a) 20 kg/m² b) 35 kg/m²

4. a) 20 kg/m² b) 22.5 kg/m² c) 25 kg/m²

WHAT ABOUT THIS? Dan, Alice, David and Paula all have a BMI between 18 and 30.

PAGES 8–9

1. a (2, 6) b (10, 6) c (13, 7) d (8, 5) e (5, 1) f (8, 1) g (9, 9) h (0, 9)

2. a) behind the right hand sofa b) on the corner table c) in or near the pot plant d) on the armchair

3. a) 4 m b) 2 m c) 4.5 m d) 1.5 m

WHAT ABOUT THIS? The perimeter would be 6 metres.

PAGES 10–11

1. a) 3 b) 18

2. a) 200 b) 90 c) 15

3. 305, but there are only 300 people in the concert hall

4. $^{13}/_{20}$ of 300 = 195, $^2/_3$ of 300 = 200. $^{13}/_{20}$ is a better estimate for the loops section.

PAGES 12–13

1. a) 11 b) $^{11}/_{36}$ c) $^3/_{36} = ^1/_{12}$

2. a) $^9/_{36} = ^1/_4$ b) $^{12}/_{36} = ^1/_3$ c) $^{11}/_{36}$

3. a) $^6/_{36} = ^1/_6$ b) $^4/_{36} = ^1/_9$ c) $^3/_{36} = ^1/_{12}$

4. a) $^{21}/_{36} = ^7/_{12}$ b) $^{20}/_{36} = ^5/_9$ c) $^{22}/_{36} = ^{11}/_{18}$

5. a) 0 b) 3 c) 1

WHAT ABOUT THIS? Suspect 3 was at the scene of the crime.

PAGES 14–15

1. a) ten past twelve b) five to one c) twenty-five past one

2. a) no b) yes c) no d) no e) yes f) no g) no h) yes

3. a) 35 minutes b) ¾ hour or 45 minutes
   c) ½ hour or 30 minutes

WHAT ABOUT THIS? Suspects 1 and 2 could
   not have committed the crime, but suspect
   3 could have done it.

PAGES 16–17

1. 80 squares

2. a) 4 squares b) 9 squares c) 9 squares
   d) 16 squares e) 2 squares

3. 40 squares

4. $^{40}/_{80} = ^1/_2$, 50%

5. a) 400 m² b) 200 m²

WHAT ABOUT THIS? It took her 17 $^1/_2$ hours to
   watch all of the camera footage.

PAGES 18–19

1. a) two o'clock b) twenty to four
   c) quarter to five d) twenty-five to seven

2. a) 15 minutes b) 70 minutes c) 35 minutes
   d) 75 minutes

3. a) talking to victims b) securing the
   perimeter c) talking to witnesses
   d) collecting evidence

WHAT ABOUT THIS? The detective has worked
   for 10 hours in total.

PAGES 20–21

1. Frequencies for men: 2, 6, 4, 2, 0, 0, 1
   Frequencies for women: 4, 0, 2, 2, 3, 2, 0

2. a) 2 b) 0 c) 2 d) 6

3. a) 2 b) 0 c) 3 d) 4

4. 2

WHAT ABOUT THIS? The suspects are a male
   in his 30s with brown hair and a male in his
   40s with brown hair.

PAGES 22–23

1. a) 11 b) 8 c) 12 d) 4

2. No men in their 40s have a degree, but
   three men between the ages of 38 and 52
   have a degree.

3. Sam Evans, Tom Collins, Toby Franks

4. Two have A levels and one of those has a car.

WHAT ABOUT THIS? There are three suspects
   with no education who own a car: Simon
   Stone, James Jones and Chris Carter.

PAGES 24–25

1. a) A 3.8 cm, B 3.5 cm b) A 12 cm, B 11.4 cm
   c) A 3 cm, B 2 cm d) A 7.3 cm, B 6.8 cm
   e) A 2.8 cm, B 2.1 cm

2. A 4.7 cm, B 4.6 cm

3. 3:12 or 1:4

4. A 3.8:12, B 3.5:11.4

PAGES 26–27

1. a) £900 b) £6300 c) £1320 d) £770 e) £1440
   f) £1680

2. a) £1953 b) £381 c) £1521

3. Simon Stone

WHAT ABOUT THIS? £79 has not been paid
   into the bank.

PAGES 28–29

1. Answers may vary, e.g. go west along St
   James's Rd, turn left and head south down
   Green Street.

2. 6

3. The suspect could be in the park or in the
   department store. He is unlikely to be in
   the police station!

4. 9

WHAT ABOUT THIS? There are more than
   20 different routes from M to P.

GLOSSARY

AREA
The area of a shape is the amount of surface it covers.

CO-ORDINATES
Co-ordinates are used to show where something is on a map or graph. They are written like this (3, 4). The first number is how far across the horizontal axis and the second is how far up the vertical axis.

DECIMAL
This type of number uses a decimal point to show amounts that are less than a whole, such as 0.7, 0.42 and 6.83.

FORMULA
A formula is a quick way of writing a mathematical rule.

FRACTION
A part of a whole. The number on the bottom (the denominator) tells you how many parts the whole has been split into. The number on the top (the numerator) tells you the number of equal parts being described.

PERCENTAGE
A percentage is a special fraction which has a denominator of 100. For example, 42% = 42/100. Per cent means 'for every hundred'.

PERIMETER
The perimeter is the length around the outside of a shape. It is measured in lengths, such as centimetres (cm) or metres (m).

PIE CHART
A pie chart is a type of graph that divides a circle in slices (sectors) of different sizes to show different amounts.

RATIO
Ratio is the relationship between two or more quantities, e.g. 3:4 which means 3 parts of one to 4 parts of another.

SIMPLEST FORM
A fraction can be written in its simplest form by dividing the numerator and denominator by the largest number possible.

TIMELINE
A timeline is a line that shows events in chronological (date) order.

INDEX